May 2016

CAREERS THAT COUNT

POLICE OFFICER

Louise Spilsbury

PowerKiDS press™

New York

Published in 2016 by **The Rosen Publishing Group**
29 East 21st Street, New York, NY 10010

Produced for Rosen by Calcium

Editors for Calcium: Sarah Eason and Jennifer Sanderson
Designer: Emma DeBanks

Picture credits: Cover: Dreamstime: Alexandru Cuznetov (top); Shutterstock: Pio3 (bottom);
Inside: Dreamstime: Blackkango 7, Kelly Boreson 26c, Martin Brayley 10, Jim Craige 11,
Dtfoxfoto 20–21, 21b, 22, 26, Lukatdb 23, Miker 12–13, Stephen Mulcahey 6r, John Roman
21t, 27, Shijianying 18, Dave Willman 1, 8, Lisa F. Young 28; Shutterstock: Arindambanerjee
6–7, Carl Ballou 14–15, Bibiphoto 5, Bikeriderlondon 17, Edw 22c, Fisun Ivan 25, Matej
Kastelic 24, A Katz 19, Peter Kim 15, Liushengfilm 10–11, 16, Stuart Monk 4–5, Jim Parkin 9,
Ramira 2, Leonard Zhukovsky 14c.

Cataloging-in-Publication Data
Spilsbury, Louise.
Police officer / by Louise Spilsbury.
p. cm. — (Careers that count)
Includes index.
ISBN 978-1-4994-0793-8 (pbk.)
ISBN 978-1-4994-0792-1 (6 pack)
ISBN 978-1-4994-0791-4 (library binding)
1. Police — Juvenile literature. I. Spilsbury, Louise. II. Title.
HV7922.S65 2016
363.2'3—d23

Manufactured in the United States of America
CPSIA Compliance Information: Batch WS15PK: For Further Information contact Rosen Publishing, New York, New York at 1-800-237-9932

CONTENTS

Which Careers Count? 4

Heroes on the Street 6

A Typical Day 8

Equipment 10

On Patrol 12

Investigating Crimes 14

Making an Arrest 16

Working with Animals 18

Traffic Cops 20

Crime Scene Investigators 22

Detectives 24

Risks and Rewards 26

Could You Have a Career That Counts? 28

Glossary 30

Further Reading 31

Index 32

WHICH CAREERS COUNT?

Who do people call when they are in difficulty or if there is an emergency? Firefighters, search and rescue officers, and lifeguards are the people we turn to in times of need. Careers such as these really count because the men and women who do these jobs save people's lives. People who choose careers like these face serious challenges, difficulties, and dangers. However, they also get a huge sense of satisfaction because they make a real difference in other people's lives.

The police officers that you see on the street spend their working lives solving crimes and helping people.

Challenging Roles

Being a police officer is a career that really counts. Police officers are the brave heroes and heroines who respond to emergencies, investigate crimes, keep the peace at public events and sports stadiums, and much more. People who become police officers thrive on challenges and they are willing to work very hard to learn the skills necessary for this difficult, but important, job.

Police officers are the first to attend the scenes of many different crimes, including robbery.

Careers That Count: A Career for You?

Here are some things to consider when you are thinking about which career is right for you:

- What are you good at? What are your interests, hobbies, and skills?
- What kind of person are you? Do you prefer to work alone or do you like to work in a team or group? Do you think you would like to do physical work or would you prefer to work at a desk?
- Talk to your teachers or a **career adviser** and find out as much as you can about jobs that interest you. Reading this book is a good place to start.

HEROES ON THE STREET

Being a police officer is a tough and **unpredictable** job. Police officers are trained to protect people from danger, and they often have to put their own lives at risk to protect other people. Police officers help the public in many different situations. They break up fights and chase **armed** criminals who are speeding from the scene of a crime in a stolen car. They patrol the streets to make citizens feel safe and they investigate crimes. Police officers are there to help others day and night, seven days a week. Being a police officer is a job that requires **dedication**, bravery, and commitment.

WHAT MAKES A GREAT POLICE OFFICER?

Many different kinds of people become police officers but they all share certain **characteristics**. These are personality features that make them suited to this important and challenging job. A police officer must be:

- **Responsible:** police officers feel a need to help others and can always be relied on.
- **Brave:** police officers are willing to put themselves in danger to save others.
- **Empathetic:** they must be able to identify with and be concerned about other people's feelings and needs.

Which of the above do you think is most important and why?

Careers That Count: Becoming a Police Officer

Police officers complete a long and careful training program before they hit the streets. To apply to become a police officer, people must be 21 years of age and have a high school diploma or an **equivalent** qualification. They must pass thorough security checks to prove their identity and their background. They must also pass a fitness check.

Police officers must be brave. Sometimes they have to control angry and violent crowds.

A TYPICAL DAY

Police officers respond to thousands of calls each year. Although no two days are the same, this is what a day in the life of a uniformed police officer might look like.

A POLICE OFFICER'S DAY

- **7 a.m.** Officers are briefed by the sergeant about assignments for the day, these may include ongoing problems they need to be aware of. They are also given areas to **patrol**.
- **7:30 a.m.** Officers do **paperwork** from the previous day's **shift**. They also check **incidents** that have happened in their area since their last shift.
- **9 a.m.** Officers start to patrol the streets in their area, by car or on foot.
- **10:30 a.m.** Officers drive to the area where a home was broken into the night before to look out for an **offender** matching a **witness** description. They also interview the neighbors.
- **2 p.m.** After lunch, officers continue their patrol. They also follow up a call about **vandals** damaging a park.
- **3 p.m.** Officers attend an accident scene where a car hit a truck. No one is hurt and vehicles are soon moving again.
- **4:45 p.m.** Back at the station, officers finish the day's paperwork and prepare a report for the sergeant, which lists ongoing incidents. When officers working the night shift take over, they will use the report to continue investigations.

Police officers sometimes visit schools to teach schoolchildren about the law and police duties.

Careers That Count: Police Officer Hours

Being a police officer is not a usual 9-to-5 job. Officers may start early and not leave until 10 p.m., or they may work night shifts. An average day can be much more **hectic** than shown on page 8, because officers have to stop patrolling and follow up on every call that comes in on their radio.

EQUIPMENT

In order to perform their jobs **effectively** and keep themselves and others safe, police officers carry a variety of tools. Many of their tools are carried on their duty belt. The duty belt holds a flashlight, a **Taser**, a **baton**, pepper spray, handcuffs, a firearm, and **magazines** or clips for reloading the firearm. Batons are used to help **restrain** an offender. Tasers give a small electric shock, and pepper spray irritates the eyes and nose. Officers use these tools to help them control **suspects**. Officers also wear a protective vest that acts as **body armor** to protect them from knife and firearm attacks.

Police carry equipment on their duty belt around their waist so it is easy to get to. This leaves their hands free to do other things.

Careers That Count: Using Technology

Officers are also trained to use important technology like two-way radios and computer systems. Police cars have computers that are linked to the station. All police car computers are also connected. The computers have instant messaging built in so that officers can talk to one another off the radio. They also use the computers to gather information about suspects.

Officers may put the equipment in their duty belts in a different order, but they always keep the most important tools within easy reach.

pistol

handcuff case

radio

magazine pouch

WHAT MAKES A GREAT POLICE OFFICER?

Officers on call must be ready to respond to any type of situation. They could be called out to search for a lost child, to stop a family argument that has become out of hand, or to stop an armed robbery. Why do you think police officers have to be prepared, alert, and ready to take in every detail of an incident at all times?

ON PATROL

Police officers on television are often shown in high-speed car chases with dangerous criminals. However, being a police officer is not just about excitement and adventures. Officers spend a lot of their time on patrol. They walk, bicycle, or drive around an area to check for signs of criminal activity. They also take time to get to know local people and local problems. This helps people feel safe.

Often, while on patrol, officers will be called to an incident in their area. The majority of the time these are **community** problems that the officer can solve without making an arrest. By listening to people and understanding their concerns, police officers can often find workable solutions to minor issues like complaints about noisy neighbors or concerns about local thefts.

WHAT MAKES A GREAT POLICE OFFICER?

Police officers need good **communication** skills. They use these to form relationships and build connections with and between people and groups. Good officers are constantly in touch with the community they serve. How might having good relationships with the community help police officers find out about issues and solve them without needing to take people to court?

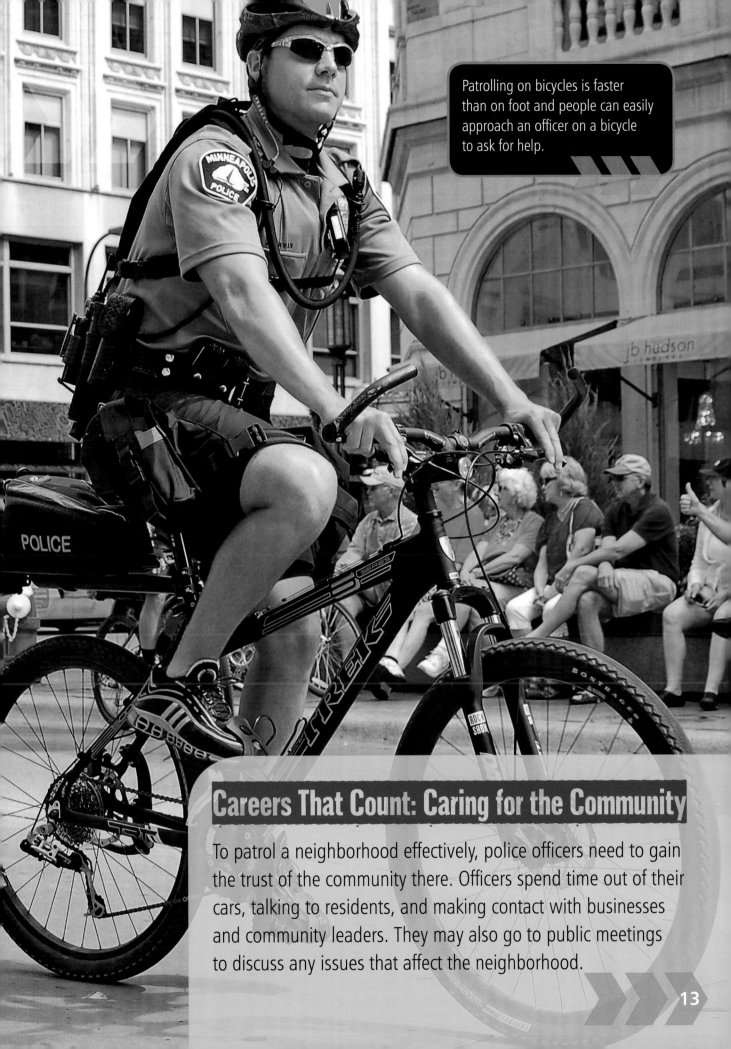

Patrolling on bicycles is faster than on foot and people can easily approach an officer on a bicycle to ask for help.

Careers That Count: Caring for the Community

To patrol a neighborhood effectively, police officers need to gain the trust of the community there. Officers spend time out of their cars, talking to residents, and making contact with businesses and community leaders. They may also go to public meetings to discuss any issues that affect the neighborhood.

INVESTIGATING CRIMES

An investigation begins as soon as someone calls the police about a crime. Police officers go to the scene of the crime and speak to the victims involved. They take details of what happened or what was stolen, if it was a robbery. They also take descriptions of what the offenders look like.

Then, officers gather together and interview witnesses. They take photographs of the crime scene, and collect and watch security footage. Police officers may also call in a scene of crime officer (SOCO), who will take fingerprints and collect other types of **forensic evidence**. Officers close off the area where the crime happened. This stops evidence from being **contaminated**. At the end of the officers' shift, they enter the crime into the crime-recording system. Officers in the next shift then have all the evidence they need to continue the investigation.

Uniformed police officers are usually first at the scene of a crime and the reports they make can be very useful in solving a crime.

WHAT MAKES A GREAT POLICE OFFICER?

Great police officers work well with different types of officers, including **crime scene investigators (CSIs)** and **detectives**. They also work with other agencies, such as the fire department. Why do you think it is important for an officer to be able to work as part of a team and understand the importance of cooperating with others?

Careers That Count: Learning the Law

Police officers are taught about different laws when they are at the **police academy**. When they become police officers, experts talk to them about new laws or changes to existing laws. They are also regularly given books with updated information about the law.

Police officers make sure no one touches anything at a crime scene, so that fingerprints found there can be used to trace the criminals who were involved.

O NOT CROSS

MAKING AN ARREST

At the end of an investigation, when evidence has been gathered and studied, and suspects have been interviewed, officers may feel they have enough **proof** to arrest a suspect.

When officers arrest a person that they believe has committed a crime, they have to explain to the suspect what his or her **rights** are. Officers may search the suspect for weapons, stolen items, or evidence of a crime. Next, the suspect is taken to the police station and booked. This is when officers record basic information about the suspect (such as his or her address and birth date). Officers take the suspect's fingerprints and photograph him or her. After the arrest, police officers pass evidence and information about the crime to the **prosecutor**. The prosecutor decides what charges should be filed against the suspect in a **court trial**.

Officers use handcuffs on the people they arrest so they cannot hurt the officers or damage the police vehicle.

Careers That Count: Paperwork

Police work does not involve active duty alone. Police officers spend a lot of time completing paperwork. They have to write detailed reports and fill out a lot of forms. They must prepare cases and evidence for others to use during a case, or for them to use themselves if they have to testify in court.

WHAT MAKES A GREAT POLICE OFFICER?

Good police officers are confident and **assertive**. When they try to arrest a suspect, he or she may resist, or fight, the arrest. Police officers must judge how best to take control of the situation and what action to take. How do you think speaking calmly and firmly and behaving confidently can help prevent a situation getting out of control?

WORKING WITH ANIMALS

Some police officers work closely with dogs or horses to carry out laws and catch criminals. K9 officers often train their dogs for one particular job, such as sniffing for explosives, electronic devices, or finding missing people. Together, officers and their dogs patrol airports, harbors, and the borders between countries. They also search prisons and vehicles. Dogs are trained to chase and catch suspects who try to escape police officers. K9 officers must have complete control of their dogs at all times.

Police sniffer dogs can be trained to find illegal substances like drugs at airports.

Mounted police officers help protect people in situations in which it would not be safe for officers to patrol on the ground. For example, they use their horses to control crowds or act as a barrier to threatening behavior at sport events or demonstrations. Mounted police are also used for patrols and to take part in ceremonies.

Careers That Count: Becoming a K9 Officer

K9 officers begin their careers as uniformed police officers. After two to four years of work, they apply for a K9 officer position. Then they take part in an **intensive** training program with a dog partner. There are only a few K9 officer jobs, so competition for them can be high.

Mounted police are police officers who patrol and carry out other police duties on horseback.

WHAT MAKES A GREAT POLICE OFFICER?

People who want to pursue a career as a mounted police officer or K9 officer need to have a real love for the animals in their care. They must exercise and care for the animals, inside and outside of work. Why do you think officers that work with animals also need to be very fit?

TRAFFIC COPS

Traffic cops are responsible for the safety of all motorists, bicyclists, and **pedestrians**. They deal with a variety of incidents, such as vehicle crashes, injured pedestrians, checking that vehicles on the road meet safety rules, and chasing stolen cars. They patrol streets, issue fines for offenses, and direct traffic.

Traffic cops are often called upon to go to the scene of a traffic incident. Officers are trained to manage the traffic when the road is blocked by an incident or accident. They examine the scene, interview witnesses, provide **first aid** for any injured people, and take written **statements** from drivers. They may also have to clear any **obstructions** or damaged vehicles, and direct traffic.

Careers That Count: Driving Skills

Drivers of police cars and motorcycles go out on patrol and can be called to incidents. These officers may have to drive at high speeds, so they are trained in advanced driving skills. These skills help them drive quickly while keeping themselves, their passengers, and other road users safe.

Traffic police are in radio contact with their station and other traffic officers at all times.

WHAT MAKES A GREAT POLICE OFFICER?

There are times when police officers and traffic officers are called to help at accident scenes and other incidents in which people are injured or killed. This can be very distressing. Why is it important that police officers can control their emotions and keep their cool at upsetting incidents?

SPEED
40

Traffic police stop vehicles for a number of reasons, such as speeding, faults on a vehicle, or dangerous or careless driving.

CRIME SCENE INVESTIGATORS

CSIs locate, record, and **recover** evidence from crime scenes like stolen cars or a home that has been robbed. This evidence can be used to help solve crimes and **prosecute** suspects.

CSIs work alongside uniformed and **plainclothes** police officers during an investigation. They wear a fully protective suit, so that things like their hair or clothing fibers are not left at a crime scene. They search for different types of evidence, from footprints and fingerprints to tools and weapons. They collect the evidence carefully so that it is not contaminated or damaged. They photograph, video, or make notes about the crime scene. They send evidence to another department, to be examined. For example, fingerprints are sent to the fingerprint bureau, where experts examine them.

CSIs check all surfaces for evidence such as fingerprints or clothing fibers.

WHAT MAKES A GREAT POLICE OFFICER?

CSIs need excellent **observation** skills. They must also be thorough and very patient. CSIs may study the same room for a long time, patiently figuring out what evidence there might be, and seeing details that other people do not spot. How do you think paying attention to detail helps CSIs collect important evidence?

CSIs wear a protective suit so they do not contaminate the crime scene. They also photograph any evidence that they find.

Careers That Count: Technology Training

CSIs are trained to use special equipment to locate evidence such as fibers, hair, and blood. They use chemical powders to reveal fingerprints and marks from shoes. They use a liquid that changes color if it comes into contact with blood. They use special lights to reveal the faintest of marks, which would otherwise go unnoticed.

DETECTIVES

Many crimes are solved by uniformed police officers. If a crime is serious or cannot be solved by patrol officers, detectives are given the case. Detectives are police officers who have been trained in investigative skills. They wear plain clothes and drive **unmarked cars**.

Detectives work with police officers, CSIs, and **evidence technicians** to solve a case. They interview suspects, witnesses, and victims, and study physical evidence as they try to piece together what happened during an incident. They work on a case until it is solved or until they can go no further with the evidence. Detectives in large police departments often specialize in a particular type of crime like homicide (murder), robbery, missing persons, or vehicle theft. This allows detectives to gain a huge amount of experience and knowledge in their crime area.

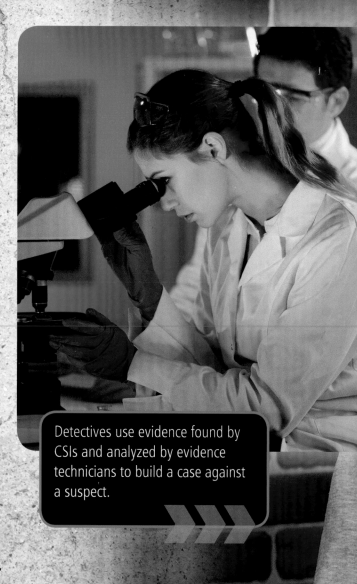

Detectives use evidence found by CSIs and analyzed by evidence technicians to build a case against a suspect.

Careers That Count: Becoming a Detective

To become a detective, officers graduate from the police academy, like their fellow police officers. Then, they usually work as uniformed officers for a couple of years, while training with a field officer. Most departments also require detectives to have an associate's or bachelor's degree in criminal justice or a similar subject.

When detectives interview a suspect they try to get the suspect to admit or confess to the crime.

WHAT MAKES A GREAT POLICE OFFICER?

Good detectives have great instincts, or gut feelings, about people and evidence, but they also have strong **analytical** and people skills. Detectives learn to read people's **body language**. For example, sweating, chewing fingernails, or turning red are all signs that someone might be telling a lie. How might reading body language help detectives find the truth?

RISKS AND REWARDS

Being a police officer has risks. It is a tough job with serious responsibilities and dangers. Police officers have to deal with angry, unpredictable people who may strike out or run away to avoid arrest. They must face oncoming, fast-moving vehicles when controlling traffic in an emergency. Sometimes, they may deal with armed criminals. However, with the proper training and equipment, most police officers enjoy a long and rewarding career.

The biggest reward for being a police officer is having a job that really counts. Every day when officers go to work, they are making life safer for people in their community. By doing so, they are making an area a better place to live. Police officers go home at the end of the day with a huge sense of achievement, knowing they have made a difference.

Careers That Count: Continuous Training

Police officers are constantly training to keep themselves safe and to stay one step ahead of criminals. They train in different types of investigations, different computer databases, and in self-defense and other policing skills. Being prepared helps officers do their job.

WHAT MAKES A GREAT POLICE OFFICER?

Great police officers are brave and always willing to do the right thing, on or off duty. They will put their life on the line for someone they do not know. They really want to serve the public and their local community. Do you think you have similar personality traits? If you do, maybe you have what it takes to become a police officer.

It feels good to make a difference! Being a police officer is a very challenging job but one that also brings real rewards.

COULD YOU HAVE A CAREER THAT COUNTS?

Do you want to become a police officer? Following these steps will help you reach your goal.

School: Join teams because teamwork is important for a police officer. Get good grades so you can go to college.

Volunteer: Volunteering with your local police department is a great place to start. However, volunteering with any community service organization can provide you with some of the skills needed to be a community police officer.

Keep fit: Join school sports teams or find other ways to exercise regularly because police officers have to be fit.

Behave: You must have a history of lawful conduct. You will need to pass a background check. Your past behavior and the choices you have made must show positive traits that will support your application to be a police officer.

College: Completing an associate or bachelor's degree program in criminal justice, law enforcement, or a related subject can help you get a job as a police officer. While not required by many departments, applicants may find a degree qualification helps them when applying for a position.

Work: Work experience prepares you for the long hours and strict rules that come with being a police officer. You do not have to do a job related to law enforcement, although that can help. Any work experience shows that you are responsible and capable of doing a job well.

Police academy: Most police officers attend some form of police academy, where they take physical and written exams to complete their training before they can enter the police force.

GLOSSARY

analytical Being able to reason and solve problems.

armed Carrying a firearm, or gun.

assertive Showing a confident and forceful personality.

baton A short stick.

body armor Clothing worn to protect people against stabbing or gunfire.

body language Gestures, facial expressions, and body movements that give clues to how people are feeling.

career adviser A person trained to help people find out which career is best for them.

characteristics Features or qualities belonging to a particular person or thing.

communication The giving and receiving of information.

community A group of people living in the same place or who share a common interest.

contaminated Spoiled and unusable.

court trial The place where both sides of a case for and against a criminal are heard.

crime scene investigators (CSIs) Police officers who locate, record, and recover evidence from crime scenes.

dedication Devoted and completely committed to something.

detectives Police officers trained to investigate serious or complicated crimes.

effectively Doing something in a way that gets results.

empathetic Having the ability to share another person's feelings.

equivalent Equal to.

evidence Documents, witness reports, and other information that can prove whether something is true or false.

evidence technicians People who help detectives collect and analyze evidence.

first aid Help given to a sick or injured person until full medical treatment is available.

forensic Scientific methods and techniques used to investigate crimes.

hectic Very busy.

incidents Accidents or dangerous events.

intensive Involving a lot of effort or work.

magazines Parts of a gun that hold bullets.

observation The act of careful watching and listening.

obstructions Things that are in the way.

offender Someone who has committed a crime.

paperwork Forms, reports, and other records that must be completed.

patrol Keep watch over an area.

pedestrians People walking.

plainclothes Not wearing uniform.

police academy The place where police officers train.

proof Something that shows that something else is true or correct.

prosecute To try to prove a case against someone accused of a crime.

prosecutor The person who oversees the case against a suspect in court.

recover To get something.

restrain To stop someone from moving.

rights Legal entitlements to have or do something.

shift A time period in which different groups of workers do the same jobs in relay.

statements Written or video recorded accounts of something that happened.

suspects People who are thought to have committed a crime.

Taser A weapon that fires barbs that give an electric shock.

unmarked cars Police cars that do not have any markings to identify them.

unpredictable Behaving in a way that cannot be predicted or known.

vandals People who spoil or damage other people's property on purpose.

witness A person who sees something happen.

FURTHER READING

Bowman, Chris. *Police Officer* (Dangerous Jobs). Minneapolis, MN: Bellwether Media, 2014.

Castaldo, Nancy. *Sniffer Dogs: How Dogs (and Their Noses) Save the World*. Boston, MA: HMH Books for Young Readers, 2014.

Herweck, Diana. *All in a Day's Work: Police Officer*. Westminster, CA: Teacher Created Materials, 2013.

Shephard, Jodie. *A Day With Police Officers* (Rookie Read-About Community). Chicago, IL: Children's Press, 2012.

Tisdale, Rachel. *Police Officers* (World's Most Dangerous Jobs). New York, NY: Crabtree Publishing Company, 2012.

WEBSITES

Due to the changing nature of Internet links, PowerKids Press has developed an online list of websites related to the subject of this book. This site is updated regularly. Please use this link to access the list: **www.powerkidslinks.com/ctc/police**

INDEX

A
accident, 8, 20–21

B
baton, 10

C
computers, 10, 26
court, 12, 16
crime scene, 14–15, 22
crime scene investigators (CSIs), 14,
   22–24

D
detectives, 14, 24–25
duty belt, 10

E
evidence, 14, 16, 22–25
evidence technicians, 24

F
fingerprints, 14–16, 22–23
firearm, 10
firefighters, 4
first aid, 20
flashlight, 10
forensic evidence, 14

H
handcuffs, 10–11, 16

K
K9 officers 18–19

L
laws, 9, 15, 18, 29
lifeguards, 4

M
magazines, 10
mounted police, 19

O
offenders, 8, 10, 14

P
patrolling, 6, 8–9, 12–13, 18–20, 24
pepper spray, 10
plainclothes police officers, 22, 24,
police academy, 15, 24, 29
police station, 16
prosecutor, 16
protective vest, 10

R
reports, 8, 14, 16
robbery, 5, 11, 14, 24

S
search and rescue officers, 4
sergeant, 8
suspects, 10, 16–18, 22, 24–25

T
Taser, 10
tools, 10–11, 22
traffic cops/officers, 20–21
training, 6–7, 10, 18–20, 23–24, 26, 29
trial, 16
two-way radios, 10

V
vandals, 8
victims, 14, 24

W
witnesses, 8, 14, 20, 24